RAILWAYS,

AND THE

WHEELS WHICH RUN UPON THEM,

BEING A BRIEF ENQUIRY INTO THE RELATIVE COST *in* MATERIAL, OF

RAILS AND TIRES,

CAUSED BY MERE *Abrasion*, TOGETHER WITH THAT OF THE LATTER, CAUSED BY *waste* IN TURNING, TO RESTORE THE *statu quo*.

Also, some Remarks on the reduced TRACTIVE power required, consequent upon the introduction of

KRUPP'S CAST STEEL RAILS AND TIRES.

By THOMAS PROSSER, C. E.

NEW YORK:
E. S. DODGE & CO., PRINTERS AND STATIONERS, 84 JOHN STREET.
1865.

RAILWAYS, AND THE WHEELS

WHICH RUN UPON THEM:

BEING A BRIEF ENQUIRY INTO THE RELATIVE COST *in* MATERIAL, OF RAILS AND TIRES, CAUSED BY MERE *Abrasion*, TOGETHER WITH THAT OF THE LATTER, CAUSED BY *waste* IN TURNING, TO RESTORE THE *statu quo*.

Also, some Remarks on the reduced TRACTIVE power required, consequent upon the introduction of

KRUPP'S CAST STEEL RAILS AND TIRES.

BY THOMAS PROSSER, C. E.

TWENTY years after the pioneer Railway had gone into operation, a very clever itinerant Lecturer wrote thus :

"It was only lately, however, that the question was raised, whether the rolling stock was really in the condition here described analagous to the permanent way, and whether there is, in fact, incidental to it, the insensible deterioration not made up by the regular annual repairs and replacement of worn-out stock ?"—*Lardner's Railway Economy*, London, p. 106. Done into plain English, this means, that railway engineers, just before 1850, did not know for certain that a locomotive would ever wear out, and require to be replaced by a new one.

It is very easy, and therefore common, for people who are *typographically* inclined, to place practical men (who are not generally afflicted with that complaint) in a false and ridiculous position, for the purpose of showing off their own sagacity, by such silly remarks of a mere empiricist.

Of the same class are those who have been telling us, with the most laughable superciliousness, during the last quarter of a century, that *the steam engine is in its infancy :* a vigorous young Hercules they admit, which has, so far, strangled all the *serpents*, in the shape of gas and water burners, and caloric engines, *ad infinitum*, which were intended to destroy it,—but *still*—an infant, and it don't appear to grow, but remains the same as it was in the time of Watt, (if even that is not paying it too high a compliment,) when, a bushel of wheat, ground and dressed in an hour, with eight pounds of coal, was one horse power. And no *improvement* (so called) has equalled that up to the present hour. A mere theoretical compilation may be a very useful and valuable production, provided it has practical experience for its *foundation*, and as this can only be obtained from experts, an author does not improve his own claim to sagacity by impugning that of such acute observers as our railway engineers must, for the most part, necessarily be.

The significance of these prefatory remarks may better appear, when, in after years, some empiricist makes the discovery, that "*it was only lately, however, that the question was raised, whether* '*steel was applicable for the axles and tires of locomotives and for rails ?*'" And, with the same self-complaisancy, we shall probably be informed, that "*its application to rail-road purposes generally is* '*in its infancy !*'" But what are the facts? Engineers and steel manufacturers well knew, many years ago, that steel was applicable to all the purposes to which it is now applied, and to many more, as is sufficiently attested by the innumerable *patents* which have appeared in all parts of the world where they are known.

All the patented inventions, aiming at the making of steel suitable for the purposes referred to, have been failures, for they have not produced that *peculiar metal* which we now *know*, and ought long ago to have *surmised* (as some probably did) from the slightest reflection, is absolutely essential to success.

Comparatively pure iron, as well as the mildest kind of steel cast (not made by cementation) are equally unsuitable, on account of being too soft, or at least wanting in stability. On the other hand, steel made by cementation, if not hard is always comparatively brittle. These are not new ideas, but such as should long ago have suggested the peculiarity required in the *metal* to make it suitable for these purposes, viz.: the toughness of the softest steel, with the stability of the hardest qualities, and combined with the most perfect homogeneousness. Whatever influence the *price* may have had in retarding its introduction, we are quite sure, now, that doubling it will not prevent its use by those who know its economic value. Besides this, the large masses of 40 tons of cast steel in one ingot, were never dreamed of, or if they were, the dreamer kept very quiet about it, probably thinking it too absurd to be worth mentioning.

Nevertheless the public history of large ingots of cast steel commenced with the Great Exhibition in London, 1851, when Mr. Krupp exhibited one weighing 4,500 lbs., the heaviest until then ever known, and led the jury to award him the *only* Council Medal granted to that class. In 1862, also, at the London Exhibition, he again exhibited an ingot which astonished every one, and distanced all competitors. That ingot weighed 20 tons, being *limited* only by the difficulties of transportation, time and space allotted. It will not do, therefore, to assign any limits to the weight of these ingots in future, seeing that they are already required and furnished of 40 tons weight, and probably may yet be required of 100 tons, and will as surely be furnished.

The *London Times* says of Mr. Krupp's Exhibition of 1862 :

" We now arrive at the consideration of one of the most extraordinary and most important collections in the Exhibition, the like of which has never previously been witnessed ; we allude to the truly magnificent display of Krupp's cast steel. The special points of interest are the wonderful soundness and the enormous size of the castings ; and in these respects he is so far in advance of all other producers of cast steel that it will be extremely difficult to approach, much more to overtake him

" The largest casting exhibited by Krupp in 1851 weighed 2¼ tons, and the largest in the present exhibition weighs 21 tons. It is in the form of a solid cylinder, about 9 ft. high, and 3 ft. 8 in. in diameter. It has been broken across to show fracture. We have inspected the fractured surface over and over again, even under a good lens, and we have failed to detect a single flaw.

" We notice drawings of locomotive axles supplied to some of our largest railway companies, and crank axles of marine engines supplied to some of our most celebrated marine engine makers. We congratulate Krupp on the pre-eminent position which he occupies in the world as the producer of the largest and soundest castings in steel."

REMARKS.—The " largest and soundest" *without* " a single flaw," is the *ultima thule* of the steel maker's hopes, and bearing upon these points a very significant compliment is paid to the Krupp cast steel, in several Patents, claiming to be for improvements in the manufacture of all others, including Bessemer's, by which they are to be made "*homogeneous*" and "*free from flaws.*"

Manufacturers saw at once that it was no ordinary cast steel which was then exhibited, but they did not know that the *large* cannon which they saw before them, possessed a greater specific gravity than is recorded of any cast steel ever before produced

The consequences of this are not fully known, but there can be no doubt that, the causes which produce it, are also mainly instrumental in producing the extraordinary stability and resilience of Krupp's *peculiar* cast steel, which no other cast steel possesses. "Resilience" is a term first applied by Dr. Young, to represent "strength and toughness conjointly;" he also defines it as, "the power of overcoming the energy or impetus of a body in motion." The term is a very comprehensive one, and is entitled to much more attention than it has usually received. There are, however, many difficulties in the way of assigning the modulus of resilience, so as to compare with metals so impure as cast and wrought iron. It should seem that, the greatest possible "*resilience*" is obtained, by any metal, when the modulus of elasticity is the same for compression as for extension,—and it may be, therefore, that the increased density of *Krupp's* cast steel over all other, produces that equilibrium therein, which we have supposed to be essential to the highest state of *resilience* (or perfection) of which it is capable.

The distinction here made, between compression and extension, is too often ignored, and both are represented by one modulus, when we know, that the ultimate disintegration of the molecular structure of all the metals, is accomplished by very different amounts of force, according as it is applied to compression or extension;—thus, copper is crushed by a force equal to one-fifth of its ultimate cohesion, and wrought iron by one-half; while cast iron requires about 6.5 times on the average, varying from about 4.5 to 8.5 times. According to the experiments of Eaton Hodgkinson, in the *Blue Book*—"Application of Iron to Railway Structures," 1849. The difference in the specific gravity of cast iron amounts to 5 per cent., varying from 7.181 to 6.839, *i. e.* one cubic foot will vary from another 342 oz.,=27lbs. 6oz. in weight,=(448.8125—427.4375) lbs The crushing force varies from 120,493 to 55,298 lbs. per square inch; while the tensile strength is from 25,775 to 11,059, and even in the same cast iron from 25,775 to 20,150 lbs. per square inch. These facts are commended to young Engineers, who put their trust in tables. The old-fashioned rule, therefore, of calculating the reliable strength of materials from their ultimate disintegration, is evidently wrong, and scarcely fit even for a *rule of thumb.* The modern method of calculation by the modulus of elasticity is doubtless better, but the imperfections of cast and wrought iron, and their entire want of homogeneousness, renders any calculation as to the amount of compression or extension which they will bear with safety, altogether unreliable.

These remarks will be fully vindicated hereafter, when we come to *contrast* the absolute *homogeneousness and integrity of Krupp's* cast steel tires, viewed under the same circumstances as cause iron ones to exhibit an entire want of both qualities, for, while the latter will sometimes almost rival the former during a short period of their service, they invariably give out long before them. And still more, it is no exaggeration to say, that iron tires of the same make and performing the same service, will sometimes run but one-fourth the distance which others will perform—such is the uncertainty of iron tires, as is well known to practical men. That the rails are subject to the same uncertain durability is equally notorious. How, indeed, can it be otherwise ? So long as action and re-action are equal, and cause and effect are equally reciprocal, there must be a ratio between the abrasion of the tire and the rail. Nevertheless, inasmuch as this ratio depends upon an almost innumerable variety of circumstances, we may not expect any great amount of accuracy in our endeavors to develop it ; for instance, if the tire is very hard and not a true circle (which is invariably the case with chilled wheels) we have a hammer, perpetually at work upon the rail to destroy it. Wrought iron tires, although equally untrue after a little wear, will hammer it less destructively (because softer) whatever may be the effect upon itself. At the same time it is self-evident, that perfect circularity in both kinds of tires, must result alike in saving both tires and rails.

It has been said (however absurdly) that the wear of tires and that of rails are complemental to each other ; in other words, that the tire which is worn the least will wear the rail the most, so that the aggregate of the two will be equal. This dictum, which has not the shadow of proof or reason to support it, appears to have been brought forward by the iron men, to save the iron rail from following the inevitable doom of iron tires into past history. Chilled wheels undoubtedly batter away the rails more than wrought iron ones, for the *reasons* before given, none of which apply to Krupps' cast steel ones. Both tires and rails of Krupp's cast steel long retain the shape originally given to them, in virtue of their stability or resistance to a crushing force, while their toughness is a guaranty against excessive grinding, and their molecular structure against lamination. It will be shown, that an ordinary wrought iron tire lost by wear 14 oz., while one of *Krupp's cast steel* lost but 4 oz., under precisely the same circumstances. Does any one believe, that, while the former actually ground the rail 86 oz., or 6¼ times its own wear, the latter could, by any possibility, have ground the rail 96 oz., for, (14+86)=(4+96), or 24 times as much as its own wear? No; it is impossible,—for, with tires maintaining their perfect circularity, and rails equally with them perfectly homogeneous, the reaction of the tires upon the rails and the road bed in one direction, and upon the rolling stock (including the locomotive) in the other, must be reduced to a minimum; and hence it cannot be too strongly insisted upon, as of the highest importance, that all the wheels of a *train* shall have such *tires*, thereby reducing also the *tractive* power required, and, of course, the weight necessary upon the *drivers*.

The *loss*, by wear, of rails and tires, by mere abrasion, is very small, as compared with the mass. A track of [illegible] will require 1,000 tons of iron, with rails of 63 lbs. to the yard; 400 tons passing over this track 60,000 times will abrade from the rails 17 tons, or 1.7 per cent. of the mass, but the rail will be used up, or at least require to be replaced, from some cause or other. That cause is not the mere abrasion, but the disintegration of the mass, caused by the severity of the service, and the increase of that mass affords no remedy to the evil, which is want of stability; the material is overtaxed. An iron wheel, carrying 100 lbs., may be run upon an iron rail for a long time without any perceptible wear to either, but, place 100 tons upon the wheel, and the destruction of both rail and wheel tire in a very short time, is inevitable.

Theoretically, the whole weight rests upon a point, but, practically, we know that there is compression, and if that compression is in the least degree permanent, deterioration has set in, and the substitution of a material having greater stability is the only remedy. The *data* for carrying out this part of the subject is very meagre, but that is no excuse for not using such as we have to the best advantage, and the more so, because of its immense importance to life and property. In doing this we shall develope some curious anomalies, while laying the foundation or more correct investigation hereafter.

The Belgium Engineer, M. Belpaire, has determined the *life* of the rail to be 120 years, with 3,000 *trains* passing over it per annum, or 360,000 trains altogether.—" *Lardner's Railway Economy*," London, page 49. Capt. Huish, of England, makes it 20 years, with 18,250 *trains* per annum, or 365,000 trains altogether.—*Ibid*, p. 51. As the calculations were made on totally different principles, they are singularly confirmatory of each other, apparently it may be, for we are not informed of the weight of the trains. The Belgium rails were of English manufacture, 55.5 lbs. to the yard, while the English rails were 70 lbs. to the yard on the average. The velocities and weights of the trains is assumed to have been proportionately greater on the English than on the Belgium lines, "so that the coincidence of the conclusions is not disturbed by this difference," says our author.—*Ibid*, p. 52. It must be admitted that this is rather loose *generalization;* however, we have to make the best of it, and hope to have better information hereafter, when the want of it is known and properly appreciated. It appears, furthermore, from the experiments of M. Belpaire—*Ibid*, pp. 49, 50,—that a 25 ton engine passing over nearly 61 miles, abrades from the rails 2.2 lbs., or 36 lbs. per thousand miles.

The average life of the *best* iron tires may be 60,000 miles, during which time four of them will grind up one ton of rails. The tires themselves will lose on the average about half as much as the rails, or half-a-ton, when they will be worn out, supposing them to have been turned twice and run three times. Of this half ton, not more than 7.217 lbs. per thousand miles is calculated to be due to mere abrasion, or about one-fifth as much as that from the rails. This, however, is but an approximation, for the uncertainty inherent in the nature of the material, as well as the service it is subjected to, renders anything like accuracy impossible.

Mr. Adams, of the North London Railway, calculates the average life of *Krupp's* tires, on that severe line, at 189,539 miles, and of Low Moor at 30,531 miles; or, as 6.2 to 1, on coupled driving wheels. But *Krupp's* had lost but ½″ of metal on the average of 21 engines, while the Low Moor had lost ⅞″. In other words, *Krupp's* cast steel tires ran 94,770 miles, and the Low Moor 8,723 miles for each ¼ "of metal lost; or, as 10,864 to 1, and there is no reason known why *Krupp's* tire should not be reduced, the same as the iron ones, by ⅞," or even more.

On the Chemin de fer de Luxembourg (France) *Krupp's* tires ran 65,774 kilomêtres (40,871 miles,) with but ⅘ths the loss by abrasion alone, of a puddled, or semi-steel one, which ran but 18,640 kilomêtres

(11,582 miles) or, as 1 to 4.117. And I am permitted to say, on authority second to none, that ¼ of an inch of a *Krupp's cast steel tire*, will outwear any thickness of iron tire.

The great defect of puddled steel, is the uncertainty of its quality, equally with iron, the interior of which latter is usually soft and does not wear as well after turning as before, and hence has arisen the vicious practice of using them without turning at all; this gives a fictitious value in their early use, for which the rails, the rail bed and the rolling stock has to suffer, in consequence of the *imperfect circularity* of the tires, which also absorbs the power of the engine to overcome it. *Krupp's* cast steel tires, on the contrary, suffer no deterioration whatever in the quality of the metal exposed to wear by turning away, while iron ones are usually considered to be half worn out, whatever their thickness, when they require turning after the first running.

The obsolete idea of flexible tires, has recently again been revived, but somewhat moderated in its ramifications, still, in any form, it must be a rail-pounding power-devouring device, which is about as rational as any other contrivance to be always going *up-hill*, when a level road is equally available. Still, if there be any economy in their use, it must at least apply, *pro rata*, to steel as well as to iron tires. It is one of those contrivances which, like hollow axles, reappears about every decade as an epidemic.

The most perfect rigidity is required in the beds of all running machines, and it would be strange indeed if railways formed an exception. Rails have been laid with a continuous support on granite blockse but as the wheels were subject to flat places, at every one of which the superincumbent weight came down upon it like a hammer; it was the same as setting an anvil upon granite instead of wood, the effect of which reacts upon the smith's arm, and soon compels him to desist from working upon it. Let us go back to first principles, by removing the wheels of a car and running it as a sled upon the rails; the parts in contact shall be perfectly hard, straight, level and smooth, and, moreover, be well lubricated;—do you not want everything as rigid as possible under the rail, just the same as under the ways of a planing machine? Now, what are wheels for, but to transfer these hard and smooth surfaces to their centres, or nearly so, to a circular form, which is easily made almost perfect, while the oiling can be done effectually and all dirt and grit be excluded, all of which are impracticable with a sled. Stop the hammering of the wheels upon the rails and a rigid road bed becomes truly economical, by reducing the power required in the locomotive to draw the load, and, of course, the weight required upon the wheels, as well as the wear and tear of everything connected with the rolling stock, rails and road bed·

It is not at all wonderful that chilled wheels hammer the life out of a rail in 3 or 4 years, which should last at least 20 under fair treatment. We learn from Mr. Winslow (M. M. of the Housatonic Railway,) that the "Reindeer," weighing 45,054 lbs., ran 72,483 miles, with an average wear by abrasion of $\frac{3}{16}''$, on a set of 4 of *Krupp's* cast steel tires. These wheel tires, which were 57.75 in diameter when they commenced running, were 57.375 in. diameter when they had run these 72,483 miles; the average width of the wear of each tire was 2¼, which gives 87 lbs.=1.49 lb. per thousand miles for a 25 ton engine, as the amount of wear by abrasion only. The wear by abrasion of the puddled steel tires on the Luxemburg, we have seen, was 4.117 times as much as *Krupp's* cast steel ones, and we are quite certain that iron ones wear much more. Hence we assign 358 lbs. for loss of metal by mere abrasion of puddled steel tires in running 60,000 miles,=6.14 lbs. per 1,000 miles with a 25 ton 4-wheel locomotive, while a former statement makes the loss of iron tires=7.217 lbs. for the same service. The amount of metal, however, which is abraded, is of little importance compared with the actual life of the rail and tire. But, we must now abandon the idea of there being any assignable ratio between them, at least in this country, for the thickness of tires is everywhere being increased, to such an extent as probably to double the life of the *Krupp's* tires on the heavy working roads, without prolonging that of iron tires at all, for, on some lines, where iron tires have been used 3 inches thick, they are not considered safe when reduced to 2 inches. We can arrive at no other conclusion than this; *the life of the rail is prolonged inversely as the abrasion of the tire.* If, now, we substitute for the iron rails, a quality of steel ones equal to the steel tires, is it not clear that the tires will be worn less in consequence thereof? If both were infinitely hard, they would not wear away at all. In pulverizing a hard substance with pestle and mortar, the latter will be abraded the same by the same service, of whatever substance the pestle may be.

The grinding of rails and tires is greatly increased by the dirt and grit which gets in between the lamina and into the pores of iron, but which cannot penetrate into *Krupp's* cast steel, for it is ground by it to an impalpable powder, with but little injury to itself.

It has been said by some of the iron men, that the *adhesion*, or *bite* of the tire upon the rail will be greatly reduced by substituting steel for iron. Surely it required no "spirits from the vasty deep" to tell us that. If there is no *grist* in the mill, there will be no grinding done. Regarding the *weight* on the driving wheels of a locomotive, and their consequent *adhesion to the rail* as a point d'appuí, it does not *necessarily* follow, that, because we reduce the grinding propensity we reduce the *useful adhesion pro rata;* but it does *necessarily* follow, that we save all the motive power necessary to perform the extra grinding. There, in fact, lies the whole *gist* of the thing. Reduce the *grinding*, and you reduce the *tractive power* necessary to perform it and in the same ratio, and you save, too, the machinery, rolling stock, rails and road bed; and if the rails are perfectly level, the wheel tires perfectly cylindrical, and both infinitely hard, with no friction on the journals of the axles, a bird may fly away with a train after the *vis inertia* is overcome, but for the resistance of the atmosphere. A-propos of axles; let any one examine the journals of iron ones, and then those of *Krupp's* cast steel, with a powerful lens, and the cause of the reduced friction of the latter, as well as the lesser quantity of oil required for lubrication will be apparent enough. An iron axle, running 70,000 miles in 2 years, is unsafe for further use; but one of *Krupp's* may be run for 50 years, or even more, according to present experience, for not one has ever been known to wear out. They have indeed run 80,000 miles without showing any appreciable wear, and the oil required is reduced to one-half of that required for iron. The best test is the fracture, which at once discloses the *cause*—of the greater density of *Krupp's* over all other cast steels, viz.: the fineness of the grain, or crystalization, and also that of its unapproachable toughness, and hence its greater *resilience* and immutability to fracture, which any tire, and particularly cast steel ones, are subject to after being worn thin.

The following table [No. 1.] comprises the most important features of the foregoing observations, in regard to the cost in material, caused by the running of a 25 ton 4-wheel locomotive 1,000 miles.

TABLE No. 1.

COST IN WEIGHT OF METAL BY ABRASION.				Total loss by abrasion and turning.
To run a 25 ton Four Wheel Locomotive one thousand miles.	Rails & Tires	Rails.	Tires.	Tires.
	Ratios.	Lbs	Lbs.	Lbs.
Iron Rails and Iron Tires................	100. to 20.	36.	7.217	18.3
Iron Rails and Krupp's Cast Steel Tires.....	100. to $4\frac{1}{6}$.	36.	1.49	2.65

The rails are put down for "abrasion" the same, whether iron or cast steel tires are used, because there is really no data on that subject. It is however impossible that such should be the case, for there is no doubt that at least half the destruction of iron rails and tires is due to the hammering force in the inequalities in the iron tires. This matter has been considered before in answer to the statement recently put forth, that the aggregate wear of the rails and tires is a constant quantity, and it was shown that inasmuch as 14 oz. of iron tires had ground up 86 oz. of iron rails, the 4 oz. of cast steel tires which had been abraded off by the same service, must have ground up 96 oz. of iron rails, or 24 times its own wear. If we apply this principle to the table [No. 1,] we shall have to make the cast steel tire grind up 29 times its own wear of the iron rails, for $29=\left(\frac{(36+7.217)}{1.49}\right)$. Instead of this result, it is confidently predicted, that the ratio of wear by abrasion between steel and steel, will be restored to the same as is obtained between iron and iron, for the difference in material has no effect upon the immutable law, that *action and reaction are equal.* If, therefore, the life of the tire is prolonged $4.8426=\left(\frac{7.217}{1.49}\right)$ times, by the substitution of cast steel for iron, there seems no good reason to doubt, that the same result will be obtained in regard to the life of the rail being increased in the same proportion by the same means, and therefore, if both are of cast steel, we may safely presume that the life of both will be increased by at least the half of the square of the previous increase, for, although we have assumed that there is perfect reciprocity in the cases, whether of rails or tires, as to the substitution of cast steel for iron, it does not apply to the substitution of cast steel rails, so far as to benefit the iron tires, because half the cause of the deterioration of both arises from the hammering of the tire upon the rail, which is not effected thereby, we therefore derive but half the benefit. Thus, $11.73=(\frac{1}{2}, 4.8426^2)$ represents the increased life of the rail and tires by substituting cast steel for iron. When, however, the rails are supported on granite blocks not more than 30 inches from centre to centre, and going down into the earth to a good foundation, below the penetrability of frost, with perfect drainage, and the ways as rigid as those of a planing machine, I have no doubt that both rails and tires of cast steel will wear quite 20 times as long as iron ones now do, that is to say, they will do 20 times the effective work with the same wear. The effective work done is the passengers and merchandize carried, the weight of which is fixed, but the vehicles for performing that service, including the locomotive may be greatly reduced: and so also of the tractive power required, and therefore the weight on the driving wheels, and consequently that of the rails. Under all the circumstances of the case, this estimate is a very moderate one, and will doubtless some day be fully realized, as defined by Era, 4, in table [No. 2]; Era, 3, is in course of development, while Era, 2, is present, and Era, 1, belongs to the past.

TABLE No. 2.

COST IN WEIGHT OF METAL BY ABRASION.

To run a 25 ton Four Wheel Locomotive one thousand miles.	Rails and Tires.	Rails.	Tires.
	Ratios.	Lbs.	Lbs.
Era 1, Iron Rails and Iron Tires..............	100 to 20	36.	7.217
" 2, " " " Krupp's C. S. Tires. ...	....	....	1.49
" 3, C. S. Rails, and " " " now..	100 to 20	3.068	607
" 4, " " " " " hereafter	" " "	1.8	.36
" 4, Ratio to Era 1.............. "	5 " 100	1.8	.36
" 3 " " " "............... now .	8.5 " 100	3.068	.607

The conclusion arrived at by table No 1 is, that one of *Krupp's* cast steel tires, will outwear seven iron ones, *upon an iron rail*, with the same loss of metal by abrasion and turning, [18.3-:-2.65]. But, if both are of the same thickness when new, the cast steel tire may be turned down, so much thinner than the iron one, as to outwear at the least ten iron ones. While, by table No. 2, upon steel rails, with all the running tires of *Krupp's* cast steel, the life of both may be calculated upon being prolonged 20 times,=[36-:-1.8]=[7.217-:-.36], as compared with iron rails and iron tires. And finally, Krupp's cast steel, when it has yielded all the service it is capable of as rail, tire or axle, requires only to be drawn out under the steam hammer to become again as available and as valuable for other purposes, weight for weight, as it was originally.

NEW YORK, *October* 20, 1865.

www.ingramcontent.com/pod-product-compliance
Lightning Source LLC
LaVergne TN
LVHW010832120826
845149LV00016B/1315

* 9 7 8 1 4 1 8 1 8 9 7 8 5 *